For that other superwoman, Sheri

Thank you to Katie Heit and Marietta Zacker
for their expertise and guidance
—D. Robbins

To my wife Michelle, with love and gratitude
—H. Aly

All rights reserved. Published by Scholastic Press, an imprint of Scholastic Inc., *Publishers since 1920.* SCHOLASTIC, SCHOLASTIC PRESS, and associated logos are trademarks and/or registered trademarks of Scholastic Inc.

The publisher does not have any control over and does not assume any responsibility for author or third-party websites or their content.

Library of Congress Cataloging-in-Publication Data available

ISBN 978-1-338-68012-6 (PB) / 978-1-338-68011-9 (RLB)

10 9 8 7 6 5 4 3 2 1   23 24 25 26 27

Printed in China   38

First edition, April 2023

Book design by Brian LaRossa

YOU ARE A STAR,
JANE
GOODALL

WRITTEN BY
DEAN ROBBINS

ILLUSTRATED BY
HATEM ALY

SCHOLASTIC PRESS ★ NEW YORK

Help!

I came to Tanzania to live among the chimpanzees.

I wanted to be the first scientist to see them eat, play, and raise their families in the wilderness.

So far, I am failing!

The chimps keep running away from me.

When I followed them up a mountain, they disappeared over the peak.

How did I get in this mess?

Believe it or not, it all started with a fuzzy little toy.

I've loved chimpanzees ever since my father gave me Jubilee for my first birthday.

Real chimpanzees are just as cute, but much harder to cuddle!

CHIMPS R US

Chimpanzees are closely related to humans, so learning about them helps us learn about ourselves. Before my experiment in the wilderness, people had mostly studied them in laboratories or zoos. No one knew how they acted in their real homes, because scientists were scared to go near them. Chimps are only four feet tall, but they're three times stronger than we are!

I grew up in England with animals all around me.

I played with a cat named Pickles and snails named Alice and Andy.

I even taught a robin to hop through the bedroom window and eat bread crumbs off my blanket!

To learn more about the natural world, I read books while sitting high up in a tree.

Stories of faraway Africa made me dream of working there as a scientist.

Could a girl like me really have such an exciting job?

My mother thought so.

She said I could do anything if I tried.

I collected a handful of earthworms from our garden.

I decided my bed was the perfect place for them to live!

GOOD OLD RUSTY

My best friend growing up was a smart black spaniel named Rusty. He taught me that animals have their own thoughts and feelings. Would you believe that Rusty loved wearing clothes? I dressed him in pajamas and wheeled him around our street in a baby carriage!

I started the Alligator Club with my sister and two friends.

We wore special badges and picked animal names for ourselves.

I was Red Admiral, named after a bright butterfly.

The others were Puffin, Ladybird, and Trout.

We made careful notes about all the plants and animals in our town.

It was good practice for studying wildlife in Africa!

I created an Alligator Club magazine with articles, drawings, and quizzes about animals.

What is a baby cat called?

Name five animals with tails.

Can you answer these questions?

THE TOADSTOOL MUSEUM

The Alligator Club made a nature museum for our neighbors. They paid to see our collection of seashells, feathers, and toadstools, and we gave the money to a charity for old horses. I was glad to help animals in need.

I hoped to study science, but I couldn't afford to go to college.

Instead, I worked as a secretary and waitress and learned about animals during my free time.

Then a letter came from Clo, an old friend who had moved to Kenya, on the east coast of Africa.

She asked if I wanted to visit her there.

I DID!

But where would I get the money for a trip?

I saved all my money from work and hid it under the carpet.

When the bulge grew big enough, I knew I could pay for my trip to Kenya!

BRING YOUR HAMSTER TO WORK DAY

Even during work, I couldn't stop thinking about animals. Luckily, my boss let me bring in my pet hamster, Hamlette, who kept me company at my desk!

My ship sailed down the Atlantic Ocean, up the Indian Ocean, and let me off in Mombasa, Kenya.

Being in Africa was the thrill of my life!

Clo showed me monkeys and springboks running free.

She also told me about a scientist who knew everything about animals, Louis Leakey.

I took a chance and visited him in the city of Nairobi.

We liked each other right away, chatting about snakes, fish, and antelope.

Dr. Leakey saw how much I loved wildlife and offered me a job.

My dream of studying animals in Africa was coming true!

I began working in the wild with Dr. Leakey, but my long hair kept getting in the way.

I pulled it back with a rubber band for my new look as a scientist. Hello, ponytail!

MEET THE MONGOOSE

I immediately started a collection of African pets. A bush baby named Levi slept under my shirt. A monkey named Kombo and a mongoose named Kip played together in my room. A fox named Chimba rested by my feet, and a parakeet named Tango hopped around on my head.

Dr. Leakey told me about a magical place where chimpanzees roamed the forests, mountains, and valleys.

It was a rugged part of Africa now called Gombe National Park, in the country of Tanzania.

He wondered if a person could live among the chimps to study their habits.

No scientist had ever done such a thing.

Dr. Leakey asked if I knew anyone brave enough to try it.

I DID!

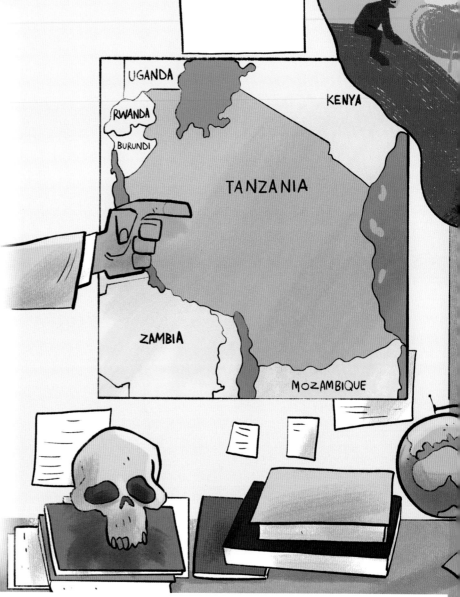

Dr. Leakey explained that it would be hard to live in the wilderness, with deadly animals, a dangerous landscape, and little to eat.

I couldn't wait!!!

A DIFFERENT SORT OF SCIENTIST

I had no scientific training, so it was risky to choose me for this experiment. But Dr. Leakey was excited to find a curious explorer who had never researched chimpanzees. He knew I might try things no one had ever thought of before.

My assistants and I set up our tents at the edge of a clear blue lake.

I headed into the forest, fighting through the thick brush, to observe the chimpanzees.

For months, I had no luck.

I tried watching the chimps from far away, but leaves and branches blocked my view.

I tried hiding near them, but they ran off as soon as they saw me.

I needed a completely different approach.

But what?

I wasn't scared of baboons, crocodiles, or other ferocious beasts in Gombe.

But when a leopard growled near my tent, I pulled a blanket over my head!

MY BIGGEST FAN

You'll never guess who joined me for the first few months in Gombe. My mother! She brought beans for us to eat, tea for us to drink, and medicine for people in nearby villages. Mum was so happy to see me working where I'd always wanted to be.

Then it hit me!

I could stop hiding from the chimpanzees.

After all, humans and chimps are
both from the same primate family.

Why shouldn't we like each other?

I sat at a safe distance and
acted the way they did.

I scratched my side.

I dug for insects.

If they seemed scared of me,
I pretended to sleep.

One day, a chimp with silver hair on
his chin looked me up and down.

I called him David Greybeard and
wondered if we could be friends.

I watched the chimps build leafy nests
for sleeping way up in the treetops.

When they left their nests for the day,
I tried lying in one myself. Sooo comfortable!

NAMES OR NUMBERS?

Scientists who studied chimpanzees always called them by numbers: Chimp Number One, Chimp Number Two, Chimp Number Three. That's because no one thought these animals had real personalities. But I could see they had their own thoughts and feelings, just like humans. So I showed my respect by giving them names like David, Flo, and Goliath.

David Greybeard could see that I was nice.

He liked having me around, and the other chimps followed his lead.

All of a sudden, I could watch them up close!

Babies rode on their mothers' backs.

Friends tickled each other.

Teenagers showed off.

I sat quietly for hours, taking notes on everything they did.

Maybe I would make a great discovery.

During a storm, a chimpanzee ran up a hill waving a stick.

That started a giant party I called a "rain dance"!

MY CHIMPANZEE FAMILY

I came to know the chimps as well as I knew my mother, father, and sister. Flo took good care of her babies, Fifi and Figan. Evered played gently with his younger sister Gilka. Goliath always made a fuss, banging on trees and shaking branches. He and David Greybeard chased each other in circles and fell over laughing!

One day, I spotted David Greybeard sitting on a mound.

He broke off a twig, stripped its leaves, and poked it into a hole.

When he pulled it out, wriggling insects clung to the twig.

He nibbled them off one by one.

To my surprise, David had made a tool.

Finally, my great discovery!

It meant that chimps were more like humans than anyone knew.

I couldn't wait to tell the whole world.

Want to know my secret to learning what chimps eat in the wild?

Studying their poop!

ANOTHER HUGE DISCOVERY

David Greybeard also showed me that chimpanzees like meat. Scientists thought they ate only plants and insects, but I saw him hunt the same way humans do. Thanks for the help, David!

Luckily, I knew all about writing articles from my days in the Alligator Club.

This time, I wrote about the chimpanzees of Gombe for a famous magazine.

Readers couldn't believe I had fearlessly lived with them in the wild.

Scientists couldn't believe a woman with no training had made such important discoveries.

I had become the world's top expert on chimps!

Dr. Leakey was proud of me.

My family was, too.

Everyone wondered what I would do next.

The magazine sent a photographer named Hugo van Lawick to film and take pictures of me with the chimpanzees.

We fell in love and got married!

BACK TO SCHOOL

I left Gombe for Cambridge University in England. I had always wanted to study science, and working for Dr. Leakey helped me pay for college. But I tried to finish as fast as possible to get back to my chimpanzee friends in the wilderness.

I hoped to turn my small camp in Gombe into a major research center.

I also hoped to have a child!

Hugo and I welcomed a baby boy and nicknamed him Grub after one of the chimps.

Grub adored animals as much as I did.

He grew up watching hyenas stroll past our tent.

How could I make the world a better place for him and every other living thing?

I learned about being a good mother from chimpanzees like Flo.

She showed me how to protect my child— and how to play with him!

FROM A TENT TO A TEAM

I founded the Gombe Stream Research Centre to continue my work with wildlife. It grew into a large operation with staff from Tanzania and other countries. Can you believe it all started with my little tent on the edge of the lake?

In my fifties, I set off on my biggest adventure: to protect people, wildlife, and the earth.

I traveled from country to country with a message of love.

We must be kind to one another and to the planet we live on.

Do you know why?

Dr. Jane Goodal

I wish I could introduce children to the Gombe chimpanzees in person.

But I can't bring them on my trips, so I bring my toy chimp instead!

Dr. Jane Goodall

SAVING THE WORLD

We can all make a difference if we try. Young people in my organization Roots & Shoots work hard to solve problems for humans, animals, forests, and oceans. What problems do you see where you live? What can you do to help?

I always remember why when I return to Gombe.

The chimpanzees are beautiful.

The valleys and streams are beautiful.

You are beautiful, too!

We must all live together peacefully to preserve our beautiful world.

Young people give me hope for the future.

So do young chimps!

I ♥ CHIMPS

The chimpanzees and I have known each other for many years. I have watched them grow from babies to teenagers to parents to grandparents. They have watched me grow, too. There's nothing sweeter than going back to Gombe to spend time with my dear friends.

AUTHOR'S NOTE

Jane Goodall has devoted herself to learning about animals for her entire life. She overcame many obstacles to pursue her passion, including a lack of opportunities for female scientists. Jane was the first person to live among chimpanzees in the wilderness for long periods of time, and she invented new ways of observing them. In her popular articles and books, she transformed our understanding of life on this planet.

Dr. Goodall's groundbreaking discoveries made her one of the world's most famous scientists. People admire her courage, creativity, and sense of humor. They also fall in love with her chimpanzee friends, who each have a unique personality.

Jane is not only a scientist but also an activist who protects animals and the environment. She founded the Jane Goodall Institute and Roots & Shoots to inspire adults and children to make the world a better place. In her tireless travels, she urges audiences to be kind to one another and to the earth. To make her point, she often lets loose a wild chimpanzee cry!

JANE'S DISCOVERIES ABOUT WILD CHIMPANZEES

- They make and use tools.

- They hunt and eat meat.

- They can be kind to one another.

- Chimpanzee communities sometimes go to war, just as human communities do.

- Mother-and-child bonds are very close, forming the heart of each chimpanzee community.

BE LIKE JANE

- Care about humans and animals.

- Be curious about everything around you.

- Be adventurous and brave.

- Work to protect our environment.

- Strive to make the world a better place in every way.

JANE'S CHIMPANZEE FRIENDS

- **David Greybeard** David was the first chimpanzee to accept Jane as an observer. He helped the other chimps feel comfortable around her, too. Soon, the two of them developed a special bond.

- **Flo** Flo was a kind mother who took good care of her offspring. She tenderly played with them, tickling the babies while dangling them from her foot. As Gombe's dominant female chimp, she made sure her family stayed healthy and happy.

- **Fifi** Fifi was Flo's only daughter. By closely watching Flo, Fifi learned to be a good mother herself. She raised confident offspring who became leaders in Gombe's chimpanzee community.

- **Figan** Flo's son Figan was one of Gombe's smartest chimps. Though small, he became the dominant male by using his brain. He and his brother Faben worked well as a team.

- **Golden and Glitter** Golden and Glitter are the rare set of chimpanzee twins to survive in the wild. They received loving care from their mother, Gremlin, and their older sister, Gaia. Golden is the brave one and Glitter the shy one, but the sisters are very close and always look out for each other.

JANE'S SPECTACULAR CAREER

1934: Born in London, England

1935: Receives a toy chimpanzee named Jubilee, named after a real chimp in the London Zoo

1947: Meets Rusty, a spaniel who teaches her that an animal can have its own mind and personality

1957: Travels to Africa to visit a friend living in Kenya; begins working for renowned archaeologist Louis Leakey

1960: Arrives at Gombe Stream Chimpanzee Reserve (today Gombe National Park) in what is now Tanzania to study chimpanzees in the wilderness; meets David Greybeard, Flo, and others in Gombe's chimp community; makes her groundbreaking discoveries of chimps using tools and eating meat

1961: Enters Cambridge University in England to obtain a doctorate in ethology, the scientific study of animal behavior

1963: Publishes an article about her chimpanzee research in *National Geographic* magazine, becoming a worldwide celebrity

1965: Founds the Gombe Stream Research Centre to advance her chimpanzee studies, support conservation, and train Tanzanian scientists

1971: Publishes her first important book about chimpanzee research, *In the Shadow of Man*

1977: Founds the Jane Goodall Institute to help people, animals, and the environment

1986: Begins traveling the world year-round to speak to children and adults about preserving our planet

1991: Founds Roots & Shoots to introduce young people to conservation

2002: Becomes a United Nations Messenger of Peace

2004: Becomes a dame of the British Empire in a ceremony at Buckingham Palace

SELECTED BOOKS BY JANE

- *The Chimpanzee Family Book*, with Michael Neugebauer. Simon & Schuster, 1989.

- *The Chimpanzees I Love: Saving Their World and Ours*. Scholastic, 2001.

- *In the Shadow of Man*. Houghton Mifflin Harcourt, 1971.

- *My Life with the Chimpanzees*. Aladdin, 1996.

- *Reason for Hope: A Spiritual Journey*, with Phillip Berman. Grand Central, 1999.

- *Through a Window: My Thirty Years with the Chimpanzees of Gombe*. Houghton Mifflin Harcourt, 1990.

JANE'S GOOD WORKS

- In 1977, she founded the Jane Goodall Institute to help people, animals, and the environment.

- In 1991, she founded Roots & Shoots to encourage young people to solve problems around the planet.

- She has worked with many organizations to champion better treatment of animals and better conservation of our natural world.

- She serves as a United Nations Messenger of Peace to advance human rights and conservation.

SELECTED BOOKS ABOUT JANE

- Edwards, Roberta. Illustrated by John O'Brien. *Who Is Jane Goodall?* Penguin Workshop, 2012.

- McDonnell, Patrick. *Me . . . Jane*. Little, Brown Books for Young Readers, 2011.

- Meltzer, Brad. Illustrated by Christopher Eliopoulos. *I Am Jane Goodall*. Dial Books, 2016.

- Peterson, Dale. *Jane Goodall: The Woman Who Redefined Man*. Mariner Books, 2008.

- Winter, Jeanette. *The Watcher: Jane Goodall's Life with the Chimps*. Schwartz & Wade, 2011.